Yes My Kid!

Addiction & Other Things You Cannot Fathom
By
John Michael Weber

John Michael Weber © 2012 IBE Ministries, Inc.
ISBN 978-1-105-59465-6

Foreword

What is wrong with my kid? Is this adolescence? Why do I feel like something is about to rock my world? Why this feeling of dread? And why am I doing everything I can to avoid rocking the boat or trying to uncover what's really going on? Denial, fear, guilt, shame, anger. Take your pick. I did. As a matter of fact, I chose each one of those excuses at some point in my quest to avoid the truth about substance abuse and my children. I quickly found out that hiding my head in the sand did nothing but give the impending storm time to gain strength.

A parent knows when something isn't right with their child. Why is it so difficult to ask for answers when it comes to our worst fears about drug and alcohol abuse? It doesn't have to be that way. "Yes, My Kid" gave me a place to hear what other parents had been through with their children. It allowed me to take what I saw in my home and compare what others were experiencing. For some parents, they might breathe a sigh of relief. I was finally able to reach the conclusion I had been hiding from all along: my precious sons were deeply involved in drug abuse.

That is not the end of the story. In fact, it is the beginning of learning helpful strategies to cope with a substance abusing child of _any_ age. "Yes, My Kid" is a weekly support group for those whose loved ones are struggling with addiction. "Yes, My Kid" is also that place where a concerned parent may come and ask questions to clarify what they may be seeing in their home. The group is a safe, nonjudgmental place to explore, in anonymity, if there could be a drug problem in your home and discover what others found helpful with their children, or just as importantly, what proved ineffective. Once a parent gets the support and encouragement they need to be healthy, they become better able to make informed and constructive choices in dealing with their children.

Lisa Benegas
Parent

Contents:

Foreword by Lisa Benegas Lombardo

Part I "Not My Kid!"

Chapter 1 Addiction

This is a book I would have never believed I would write, but then God takes me in directions I thought not possible all the time. First of all, whatever you have heard about addiction, whatever you have heard about ADHD, Bipolar Disorder and any other mental defects, I encourage you to gather them into one file in your mind and then put them in the recycle bin of your brain. Don't delete them; just keep them inactive while reading this book. Got them filed away? Good, now with a clean chalkboard let's take a journey.

I was curious as to what makes a person an expert in any given endeavor so I looked up the definition online and Merriam-Webster has this to say:

: One with the special skill or knowledge representing mastery of a particular subject

Now at first the word "mastery" threw me for a loop. I possess a special skill (I am an addict, been there and lived it and learned how to deal with it, not master it), I also have a wealth of knowledge from the above experience as well as studying the subject of addiction. All this put together makes no one an expert in the field of addiction, at least not by definition, for that presumes I have mastered the disease and that is not possible.

So with an opened mind, and an open heart we will together travel to places you have never been so that you may have an explanation as to why your loved one does what is inconceivable to you, to carry on with their drug abuse or drinking. *From this point forward if the word drug is utilized, it includes alcohol.*

First rattle out of the box I am going to give you my theory on how addiction comes about. This theory is compiled from my own experience as an active addict, from some 15 years of observation of addicts like me both active and in recovery and from working with licensed therapists for just around three years.

Problem here...

The brain defies explanation. The good news is we have gained leaps and bounds in studies of brain. We can now look at the brain imagery and define how and what certain drugs make the brain react. This is all good but how does the brain get there in the first place? Truth be told, there are many theories and arguments on both sides of the disease concept. I am going to cut through those arguments and simplify the birth of addiction as I have learned, experienced and observed.

The brain is the "mother board" of the human anatomy if you will. It controls everything and for the most part, the brain has the same basic functions in all people, with variations of course, but one could say we are created equally. We are not, if we are addicts. The computer analogy would be that addicts are hardwired differently, with a Trojan virus and the addict's brain is high speed internet without a "pop-up blocker." You could, if you like, read for days, information on why this might be true. Studies across the board believe that this hard wire malfunction is sixty percent genetic. That leaves forty percent of unknown catalysts that might birth a baby into addiction.

Suffice it to say and addict is born that way. Parents will not see this because the addict baby is just as cute and curious as any other. What we know now about addiction can give parents a heads up that their child might be predisposed to addiction as evidenced by their family tree, but what parent wants to give reality to that horrible thought as they cradle their new born gift from God?

Imagine it as a hot wire that leads to a switch for a fan in the brain. As long as that switch remains off, the brain can function without interference from the breeze the fan would cause. In other words, the addict still is not wired properly, but leave the switch off and they can maneuver around any obstacles their brain disorder throws at them.

A child's development years are considered to be from two to four years old. What this means is that their brain is a sponge gathering the information they need to determine if they are loved and how the world will view them and what they will do to cope with all the information they gather. The formative years are usually when that switch to the fan gets flipped to the on position.

Take for example an orphan in a "baby mill." Those babies are kept alive but, in many cases, in their first two or three years they are in a crib getting fed, not when they're hungry but as necessary. They get their diapers changed, not when needed but on a schedule. They cry and no one comes. Before they can say "momma" or "daddy" they have decided the world sucks and so do they. They know not love and it will be years of therapy before they ever do, if they ever do.

Recent tests show that seventy-five percent of teens that use drugs, experienced an early trauma in their lives. I am going to step it up and say that all addicts experience some sort of trauma in their formative years that act as a catalyst and flips the fan switch. Let us examine what a *trauma* is defined to be.

The Longman Dictionary of Contemporary English offers the following:

1. **An unpleasant and upsetting experience that affects you for a long time.**
2. **A mental state of extreme shock caused by a very frightening or unpleasant experience.**

Now, dear ones, what we cannot determine is this, what does a baby perceive to be traumatic? What is traumatic to an adult would certainly not be the same as what a baby would consider to be traumatic. A step further would be to surmise that what a "normal" baby would consider business as usual; a baby addict would ingest the same event as traumatic.

Studies show that an addict experiences pain five times the level of a "normal" person." The upside is that an addict experiences pleasure at the same escalation. Sounds bipolar, does it not? So there is a baby in a crib and the stars are aligned just right for the switch to be flipped and a door slams somewhere in the house and for whatever reason, this becomes an event that the baby cannot reconcile and cope with and then the switch is flipped and what may have been settled in their precious little brains gets blown all over the place by the fan and the chaos begins.

As the child grows it stands to reason that the problem grows as well. With no realization by parents or friends that the problem is even there, it grows unchecked. The addict child may very well exhibit exceptional abilities in areas of school work, athletics, music and other activities and this brings on praise from all as to how well they are doing. To the contrary the child begs to differ, silently, for fear that they must surely be insane to be so uncomfortable in their own skin when the world heaps nothing but praise upon them. This creates a conundrum in the sense that they are damned to ridicule if they come clean with their insecurities and damned to death if they don't. So they cope as best they can.

Every child has peers. In the beginning of social activity, even with "normal" children the angst that accompanies their introduction into a society of their peers is at best, uncomfortable. For the addict it is downright horrifying. All species of mammals gravitate to those most like themselves and so is true of the young addict and eventually one of their peers is going to utter the most dangerous of suggestions, "Hey, try this." So they do and all of a sudden the world rights itself. The chaos dissipates and all is well. Gone is that insecure child. Gone is that low self esteem. Gone, dear ones, is that child you once knew.

Now that the child has found the correctional device for their madness the only problem is the alcohol or drugs wear off. The trick is to stay on top of that and kill the pain before it arrives. At your average teen party, for instance, a teen who occasionally abuses substances, will have a drink or two or a blunt or two after getting to the party and begin to feel buzzed. The addict teen will have the same amount before the party and not get buzzed; they will reach a pseudo normality that makes them comfortable enough to even go to the party.

In the meantime, the problem they got in the developmental years or better stated at birth, continues to grow. The larger that problem becomes, the harder it becomes to mask it so the intake of the solution they have discovered increases. And so on, and so on, bigger problem, bigger drugs. No one notices for many reasons. At first the child maintains their grades. Their mood swings are attributed to just being a teenager. They are developing manipulation tools without being conscious that they are becoming the greatest of deceivers. They have crossed the line from abuse to addictive use.

This is the point where it becomes noticeable to the world that the drugs are a problem and causing, as Alcoholics Anonymous so aptly describes in the first step, their lives become unmanageable. This is when parents become either part of the solution or add to the problem. There are so many dark clouds in society that follow the topic of drug abuse that recovery gets dealt a bad hand. The lack of understanding the disease worldwide brings with it many myths and statements that are quite simply untrue. One of them is a parent's immediate inclination to say, "Not my kid."

As a counselor I have dealt with many parents and the majorities of them are much easier with the diagnosis of Bipolar Disorder, ADHD, depression and chemically impaired than they are with accepting that their child is a drug addict. I can only surmise that one of the reasons this is true is that the afore mentioned ailments can be balanced by medication, ironic is it not? The other reason is the horrible stigma that is a parasite to drug addiction.

When and if the parents get onboard with the fact that their kid is an addict a whole new set of problems occur. No parent wants this problem or any problems with their offspring, but when they do occur, the first response is, "Where did I fail them?" Allow me to let you off the hook. If what I say is true and many agree with me that are much more scholarly than I, then I maintain that even if you weren't the best parent in the world and even if you might have been the catalyst that flipped the fan switch, it is still not your fault. It was going to happen somewhere, sometime and there was not anything you could have done to prevent it when you did not have any clue of it existence in the first place.

All that being true, if you did what any decent parent would try to do and in the formative years instilled in your child a moral compass, a good sense of right and wrong and hopefully a belief that there is a God or, for those of different beliefs, a sense of mother nature or some power greater than us, then that is as engraved in your child's psyche as the addiction is and will play a huge role down the road they trudge.

Proverbs 22:6 Train up a child in the way he should go, And when he is old he will not depart from it.

Chapter 2 Yes My Kid

When you arrive at the point where you can no longer deny that your child or loved one has an issue with drugs then you can implement a plan of action. I will list suggestions that are simple and proven but extremely painful and difficult to put into action.

- First, one should consider an intervention. If you have watched television and seen "intervention" try and put that in the recycle been with the other stuff you are storing. Gather your family, close family that is and it is highly recommend you get a party to mediate that is not emotionally wrapped up in the drama that has become your life. This person could be a drug counselor, a member of AA with 12 Step experience or clergy that has experience with such things. Gather the troops and set up a plan of attack.

- Secondly, set things in place for options. Research the local recovery centers and see if there are openings and be honest with them about what you are planning. It does one no good just to get your loved in a room and say, "Hey you're messed up and we know it." You are going to present them with two options and just two. The first option is they can go into a rehab and as long as they are making an effort to change, they have your moral support. The second option is that if they refuse to go, there are no more options and they no longer, even though you love them, have your support in anyway.

- If they agree, get them immediately into a rehab that has a detoxification unit or to the hospital for detoxification and arrange transfer from the hospital directly to the rehab.

- If they pick option two, ask them where they would like to be dropped off and then turn them over to your mediator to drop them off somewhere.

Simple and tough, right? You are right, but I can tell you from my own experience, that as long as the consequences of my actions were minimal, so was my effort to change. The above steps are great, but what if you have an adolescent? Well then the issues become far more complicated, sorry.

My drug abuse began at home. I am not blaming anyone, just stating the truth. I had been given sips of dad's beer, shots of tequila by another family member at 13 and I began taking pills from mom's medicine cabinet around 13 years old. They had no clue what the outcome for me would be at that time. I am here to take that particular excuse away from you.

16

There are tons of issues in dealing with adolescent drug abuse. In addition to the possibility that they are an addict with all the chaotic electrons being blown around their young brains, they have the normal angst of being a teenager with raging hormones and every move they make they are thinking, "How am I doing?"

Parents are going to become much more knowledgeable about legal issues. They will learn more about drugs and the lifestyle that surrounds them than they ever wanted to know. They will know more about health insurance than the senate and congress know. Parents of teens will have their worlds flipped upside down, so better to prepare for that than allow it to catch you by surprise.

It is extremely important that parents, even divorced parents, get on the same page on how to deal with their child. A divided front is a young addict's best tool. They will play you against each other in ways you cannot fathom. If they see that you are united, you put a serious road block on their road to addiction. So however you proceed, be united.

It is difficult to find therapists willing to take on teens. More difficult to find programs that adhere to treating the youth, but they are out there. It is good if you are comfortable on your computer and the phone because you will be utilizing both more than you thought possible. A parent has a lot of homework to do because, like anything else, there are good facilities and bad ones.

It is imperative that you remember that you are the parent. It is your home in which they dwell and it will be your rules they must follow, lest they suffer the consequences. Understand dear ones, that no matter what you do to slow them down, they will find a way around the stumbling block. This doesn't excuse you from stacking those blocks against them.

Consequences are obviously going to be different for teens. If they have a car, take it away, this is the equivalent of cutting off their legs. Without driving privileges they fall in the ranks of importance amongst their peers. Take their phone away; you are probably paying the bill anyway. They will replace it with a pay as you go but you just added another difficulty factor in keeping their addiction running. That X-box, donate it to needy children. My point is a parent must hit their child where it hurts.

Check your refrigerator and your medicine cabinets. Keeping alcohol around is just plain irresponsible when living with an addict. Your medicine cabinet is a smorgasbord for an addict. If you must be on prescribed medication, lock it up. Don't pretend to know which drugs are ok and which are not, lock them all up. Don't leave your wallet or your purse lying around, you will find them missing money you thought you had and at first you will shrug it off like you must have been mistaken. Odds are great that a twenty is missing not because you miscounted but because your child lifted the money. By this time folks, the child has every bone in their body and their mind screaming to use drugs. They will do what it takes to quiet the scream.

The process by which you choose a recovery venue for your child is very important. I must give my fellow Christians a word of caution, actually a few words. I recently met a pastor who said that from the cradle he never had a problem believing in Jesus, he did not, however; have a clue as to how to quit drinking. He now incorporates the 12 Steps of AA into his sermons. My point is, just like you cannot force your child to get clean and sober, you cannot force Christ on them either, please leave that between God and them.

Yes My Kid

Chapter 3 Parental Recovery

Parents and loved ones often believe that they don't have a problem, "my son has the problem, not me." If you don't know this by now, *you* do have a problem. Any loved one of an addict needs recovery and best they understand this even before whomever they love realizes they need recovery. Easy to preach, harder to hear and borderline impossible to take action on this simple cliché', "Let go and let God."

Still it is vital that one reach that pinnacle at some point, that they may have some inner peace and be able to deal with their loved one both in and out of recovery. One cannot give away something they do not first possess. Anything less achieved drags everyone down, so let us now look at how on earth the loved one of an addict copes with someone who has no copping skills at all.

When you come to terms with, "Yes, my kid has a problem," it is time for you to seek help, not for your son, your husband, your wife, your mom or dad, no it is time for you to seek help for you. Support groups are a gift from God, utilize them. IBE Ministries, Inc. has developed one called, you guessed it, "Yes My Kid," and we will explore more on that in part two of this book.

Alanon is an excellent resource. I encourage all of you to read up on the history of Alcoholics Anonymous for it is a miracle of great proportions. From that group, Bill Wilson's wife had to keep the wives of drunks entertained and they found that by sharing the struggles experienced with their husbands they created a spiritual, emotional and productive bond with each other. That was the beginning of Alanon.

Celebrate Recovery is another resource I recommend. This offers support to addicts and loved ones under the same roof. They start with praise and worship and perhaps a testimony of a person who has, with God's help, overcome addiction or their loved one who is addicted. Following that separate rooms in the church are provide for all types of recovery.

For those who are not Christian I strongly recommend Alanon as opposed to Celebrate Recovery unless you are quite sure you can be open minded for if you cannot, any mention of God or Jesus will just give you an excuse to say it doesn't work. Alanon provides a program that is less religious and more spiritual in nature.

Personal counseling is highly recommended. You can tell therapist things that are not meant for an open forum that Alanon and other support group's offer. There are no doubt certain happenings or events or even thoughts that you have locked in a vault have sworn to take them to your grave. With a therapist you grow to trust, this vault must be opened and its contents dealt with. Trust me when I tell you that you will not shock a therapist with confessions of the soul. The truth will set you free but getting to the truth might hurt. If you want to have peace in your heart, mind and soul, you will need to be open minded and willing to change.

Chapter 4
Contempt Prior to Investigation

"There is a principle which is a bar against all information, which is proof against all arguments and which cannot fail to keep a man in everlasting ignorance—that principle is contempt prior to investigation."
—Herbert Spencer

That quote can be found on page 568 in the book <u>Alcoholics Anonymous</u>. It is now relegated to Appendix II but used to be in the personal stories and spoke to the idea of a spiritual awakening and belief of a power greater than us or perhaps more aptly put a "God Consciousness." It has survived all editions of the book and there is evidence that it appeared even before Herbert Spencer coined it in the 1800's. That principle is one that personally, continually keeps me on the watch for practicing said contempt.

Time for you to get a little closer to God, as you understand Him. You are going to need all the help you can get and who better than your God and Creator to navigate these stormy seas of addiction. **Step 1,** "We admitted that we were powerless over our (son, daughter, boyfriend, girlfriend, husband, wife, mother or father) and that our lives had become unmanageable.

No parent wants to concede that they are powerless over their child, not now, not in Biblical times, i.e. the Prodigal Son. Let us take a look at that parable for a moment because even if you are not a Christian, this story has a few points and principles that are applicable today. Good time for us to remember that contempt prior to investigation bodes not well for anyone.

Luke 15:13-16 "Not long after that, the younger son got together all he had, set off for a distant country and there squandered his wealth in wild living. After he had spent everything, there was a severe famine in that whole country, and he began to be in need. So he went and hired himself out to a citizen of that country, who sent him to his fields to feed pigs. He longed to fill his stomach with the pods that the pigs were eating, but no one gave him anything."

Does this ring true in the present? Absolutely, how many teenagers think they know what is best and cannot wait to get released from the "bondage" of their parental care? Now a drug addict, will if allowed to mind you, eventually find they are eating the crumbs from swine in some urban alley or suburban field and have a moment of clarity as to just how well off they were before drugs.

The difference for the addict is, he will long to be home where he can do drugs comfortably and many parents, well intended as they may be, put a revolving door on this comfort zone and here's the word you have been waiting for, you **enable** your child to continue on the path of destruction.

By enabling your child or loved one, you are just delaying what is inevitable. An addict has to reach the point where, "The pain becomes greater than the fear of change." I don't know who to credit that quote to except for a friend in AA we called Reverend Dwight said it all the time and I keep it close. Enabling an addict will be the most costly investment of your life. Marriages break up, financial ruin, emotional trauma and years of therapy are the products reaped by those who enable. And then you might have another child, what about them?

Luke 15:28-30 "The older brother became angry and refused to go in. So his father went out and pleaded with him. But he answered his father, 'Look! All these years I've been slaving for you and never disobeyed your orders. Yet you never gave me even a young goat so I could celebrate with my friends. But when this son of yours who has squandered your property with prostitutes comes home, you kill the fattened calf for him!"

Can you blame that son for his outrage? How many sons and daughters get lost in the drama of trying to save the one who went astray? All kids desire their parent's approval and even their pride in them. They do the next right thing and get nothing but teary eyed parents concerned about the missing child. I am not saying that one should not welcome home the lost lamb, but while they are gone do not neglect the ones at home. Let God worry for the lost and you embrace the ones at home so that the return of the prodigal will be celebrated by the whole family, rather than being resented by those who have met life on life's terms all along.

Part I Wrap Up

I have pointed out some problems you will face with addicts, which is the easy part. In Part II I will give my best effort at solutions. As a summary on Part I, let me tell you that you are not alone in your confusion, fear and worry about drug addiction. It is the only disease that works hard at convincing everyone that it does not exist. Addiction is quite successful at this because our government can't seem to make up its mind whether or not addiction is a disease. For every medical argument that it is a disease there are as many that say it is not.

"He complained in no way of the evil reputation under which he lived, indeed, all over the world, and he assured me that he himself was of all human beings the most interested in the destruction of Superstition, and he avowed to me that he had been afraid, relatively to his proper power, once only, and that was on a day when he had heard a preacher, more subtle than the rest of the human herd, cry in his pulpit, "My dear brethren, do not ever forget, when you hear the progress of lights praised, that the loveliest trick of the Devil is to persuade you that he does not exist."
Charles Pierre Baudelaire from the short story, "The Generous Gambler"

And the same is true of drugs.

Part II Take the Steps

Chapter 5 Why Me?

Matthew 7:3 *And why do you look at the speck in your brother's eye, but do not consider the plank in your own eye?*

The verse above is Jesus saying; don't judge, you got your own issues. In AA they say, clean up your side of the street. So why you? Because you now have some serious baggage even if by some miracle, you had none before your loved one was found out to be an addict. No one is immune, make no mistake.

So in order to help someone, one has to possess something within to pass on. If a person is angry and reaches out to an addict, who is angry by mere existence, then both will be angrier than before. I would find it difficult to take marital advice from a recently divorced therapist for example. Don't try and clean up a mess while standing in the middle of it, that is a futile exasperation of time, energy and it will drain both you and the would be recipient of your good intentions gone bad.

I personally recommend the 12 Steps of Alcoholics Anonymous because, short answer, they work. That being said however you choose to change it is important to know that the only thing that needs to change is everything about you. This change occurs as the result of a wakening of your spirit. Those awakenings require the Steps or the equivalent because in Christian terms you have died spiritually and are in desperate need of a rebirth. I am really a "buzz-killer" aren't I?

As counselors we are only able to draw blood by telling you the truth. You, dear ones, have to ask for the band-aid. So I am going to remain in "buzz-killing" mode for a while longer and pray that you eventually request the band-aid. To do this I must divide to conquer, so I must address dads and husbands, then mothers and wives. Both sexes should read about each other so they can hold each other accountable. Here we go!

Dads, Husbands & Other Male Species

OK men, time to "man-up!" probably not like you are used to though, when I say "man-up" it doesn't require physical prowess or taking a bullet or anything that tests your testosterone. This process is going to require you to admit you cannot do this alone and that is tough for most men to swallow. We're still in the dark ages, us men, a time when we thought we could handle anything that was relevant to our kingdom. Terms and phrases like, "shake it off," "tough it out," "pull yourself up by your bootstraps," and my favorite of all, "kids are resilient," have to be filed in the archives for now and for all time for they do not hold water.

For those of you men that have built a comfortable empire and think you can buy your loved ones sobriety, you cannot. You can put pen to as many checks to as many rehabs as you deem, in your stubbornness, to be necessary and your empire will crumble and your loved one will be more strung out than when you first bailed them out. Writing the check and thinking you're contributing to the betterment of your child or spouse is a fallacy and best you recognize that now before your Rome burns to the ground. If you are reading this and thinking, too late Rome is ashes, fear not there is still hope.

Get up, take your macho card out of your wallet and leave it home and find a support group. The ratio in support groups and in my own practice for men to women is severely unbalanced. My personal experience is that seventy-five percent of people that show up on behalf of their child are women, the man is at home. The same would be true for wives versus husbands. Men have that attitude of, "we can handle this; I don't need counseling or some support group." Standing alone against addiction is a tragic as being in the addiction itself. Become willing to change your perspective guys, because trust me, the money will run out, marriages break up and on and on, you will not know what hit you.

So men, this is not a simple issue that can be solved with the color inside the lines techniques. Step back and take a serious look at what you bring to the table. If you are honest you will most likely find that changes could increase your value of being a true head of the household and one of the hardest things for a man to accept is something he can't fix. There is no shame in running up against a problem that you need to seek help on but it is disgraceful to continue, business as usual, when you know you need the help but your pride keeps you from asking.

Finally, your family is looking to you for direction. The path you lay out will be followed as long as progress is being made but the minute that pride prevents any progress, your house will be divided and your spouse will seek the help on her own, for the love of her child, trumps her duties as a wife. Take the first step; admit you are powerless over your loved one and their addiction and that it is making your life unmanageable. Until you can get wrapped around that idea, you will be spinning your wheels.

Moms, Wives & Other Female Species

You are all women and I have many times heard you roar. Mothers are the most willing to seek help and the most unwilling to accept what is suggested. Still, they show up in hopes of getting their child or their husband fixed whatever it takes as long as it doesn't hurt too much. I have run many mothers off with one session because they are so tethered to their child by an umbilical that had never been severed and they were not about to allow me to suggest that the chord be cut.

So women, hear me roar. Let us look at what it is we desire for the children and loved ones of an addict. If we are speaking of your child, certainly what you want is for them to be happy, right? If you are a wife and your husband is addicted, you would desire to have in your life the man you fell in love with returned to you, right? If I told you that the best way to achieve these desires would be to let them go and work on you, would you continue to listen or be polite and bolt?

Lord please forgive the mothers for they know not what they do. Here is an observation, I have run into many, many mothers who would rather have their child be Bipolar or have an ADHD diagnosis, or some other mental ailment than accept the mere suggestion that their child is an addict. In fairness, society has taken a scarlet letter and stamped addiction with it so that an addict is shunned and relegated to those ranks just above lepers.

Let us look for a moment at Bipolar disorder. Before 1980 this diagnosis was termed manic-depressive. I found in my extensive research, by extensive I mean I went to caregiver.com, and discovered that this ailment of the gray matter, known as the brain, has been around for centuries. Jules Falret coined term "folie circulaire" (circular insanity) in 1854, and established a link between depression and suicide. Circular insanity, I can relate to that because it describes me.

Here's my point, I have not met a fellow addict on the road to recovery who is not Bipolar. Why do you think we did drugs in the first place? It certainly was not because we were mentally balanced and wanted to throw a wrench in the gears. On the contrary, addicts are far off balance and the drugs, for the moment, removes that wrench that is blocking the gears. Again, the drugs and alcohol or not the problem they are the solution to a mental disorder that affects all addicts. So if you want a diagnosis for your child that suits you, call them Bipolar or whatever you wish, you have to accept that until now, they have dealt with that by taking drugs to quiet the mental madness.

Here is something else women, addicts lie and they are skilled liars. That creates this problem, let's say your child is diagnosed with ADHD and put on Adderall. The psychiatrist will grill your teen on other substances they might be using and your teen will lie and so the doctor treats them as if and prescribes the amount and dosage to the child based on a clean slate to work with. All the while your child may have been self medicating the ADHD unknowingly and so the Adderall is going to be confused and not perform and the doctor prescribes more and so on. Circular insanity if you will.

ADHD and Bipolar disorders are very real and need to be treated as such. My point is until you get your child or your husband for that matter, off their own self diagnosis and self medication, treatment for the brain disorders will not work.

Back to you ladies, you have to be willing to step back and take a look at yourself. How can you better serve the well being of your loved one? By letting them go. Say this out loud, "I have to let them go!" Or your can do the tried and proven prayer of prayers for serenity:

God, grant me the serenity
To accept the things I cannot change,
The courage to change the things I can
And the wisdom to know the difference.
Living one day at a time;
Enjoying one moment at a time;
Accepting hardships as the pathway to peace;
Taking, as He did, this sinful world
as it is, not as I would have it;
Trusting that He will make all things right
if I surrender to His Will;
That I may be reasonably happy in this life
and supremely happy with Him
Forever in the next.
Amen.

Ok, ladies and gentlemen, time to get busy!

Chapter 6 Helpful
HINTS!

If you follow me thus far and agree that you must change, bravo! This will not be easy, no, not at all. So we can start slow. If we want to make big changes we must be able to handle small ones at first. Mark Twain said, *"The only thing that likes change is a wet baby!"* Mr. Twain nailed that did he not?

You are awake if you are reading this which is to assume at some point tonight you will go to bed and no doubt you will be worried to death about whoever was the catalyst for you reading this in the first place. So here is a small change you can make and it is simple. If you normally get into bed on the left side, tonight enter from the right. Continue this every night until it doesn't bother you anymore.

How do you pray, what do you ask God for, what do you thank Him for and do you believe He is listening? Here's what I do and even if you don't believe in God, fake it, but I simply go through my day with Him, it is what AA calls a 10th Step inventory or checklist. It is a great way to go to sleep just you and God talking. You can tell him you are mad, you can tell him you are mad at him, you can tell him you don't deserve this agony but my suggestion is you seek to be at peace with whatever God is up to and that you awaken the next day to a brighter situation.

In the morning, change something. If you drink coffee before getting in the shower, reverse that, the coffee will still be there. You no doubt have a set way of driving to work, unsettle it and go a different way; you would be surprised how you view things differently when you try doing something different.

Here's a tougher one, if your loved one is out carving deeper the path of destruction they are on and they call, don't answer. Let it go to voice mail. If they text, save it and read it later. Addicts are really good at what they do, if we need money we are going to the softer easier source of manipulation first, that would be you, and if we cannot get through, we move on to choice two and so on. You need not worry about your loved one's street savvy for that was in place a long time before you even had a hint they were a mess.

Make a commitment everyday to get to a support group, counselor or lacking that, you get out with a group just to have a little break. Treat yourself to that thing you have wanted to do for awhile but because of life, have not gotten around to as yet. Talk to God all day, always keep the line of communication open and again, if you're not quite on board with God, fake it still.

Hopefully you get the idea, make small changes and then when the time comes you will find you have made major changes without even knowing. We are going to walk through the 12 Steps now; this is where you can become active in your recovery. These steps allow you to find the very best in you and to face up to and disown the very worst on you. This is a pass on being selfish, for right now, it is you and you alone you should be concerned with.

Below is a 10th Step Checklist utilized by many alcoholics and it can be helpful to you when talking with God at the end of a day:

Checklist:

- **Conscious Contact**

    o **Did I start my day with a conscious contact with God as I understand Him?**

    o **Did I start my day with "Please"?**

    o **Did I start my day asking for guidance?**

- **Did I try to be pleasant to everyone?**

- **Did I go out of my way to be kind or to do a good deed for someone?**

- **Did I demonstrate gratitude in my life?**

- **Did I totally reject resentment?**

- **Did I resist the PLOMS? (Poor little old me's)**

- **Did I indulge in any _____? (your favorite character defect)**

- **Did I resist the temptation to gossip or criticize?**

- **Did I have support group contact today? (reading, phone, or meeting)**

- **Did I renew at any time during the day my conscious contact with God as I understand Him? (a quiet time, a meditation break)**

- **Will I close my day with "Thanks"?**

    It is a comfort to have that all day all night accessibility with God. Try it and you will be surprised.

Chapter 7 Miracle Steps

I personally believe everyone should own a copy of the book <u>Alcoholics Anonymous</u> or as we insiders call it, the "Big Book." If you feel yourself too Christian to use terms like "Higher Power" I respect that and would refer you to the <u>Life Recovery Bible.</u> Better idea is to get both and see how closely they mesh.

AA Steps

1. We admitted we were powerless over alcohol - that our lives had become unmanageable.

2. Came to believe that a Power greater than ourselves could restore us to sanity.

3. Made a decision to turn our will and our lives over to the care of God as we understood Him.

4. Made a searching and fearless moral inventory of ourselves.

5. Admitted to God, to ourselves and to another human being the exact nature of our wrongs.

6. Were entirely ready to have God remove all these defects of character.

7. Humbly asked Him to remove our shortcomings.

8. Made a list of all persons we had harmed, and became willing to make amends to them all.

9. Made direct amends to such people wherever possible, except when to do so would injure them or others.

10. Continued to take personal inventory and when we were wrong promptly admitted it.

11. Sought through prayer and meditation to improve our conscious contact with God as we understood Him, praying only for knowledge of His will for us and the power to carry that out.

12. Having had a spiritual awakening as the result of these steps, we tried to carry this message to alcoholics and to practice these principles in all our affairs.

There they are folks, what I like to call the 12 Steps to Heaven or the 12 Steps from the gates of Hell. I have heard the steps summed up in six words: "Trust God, clean house, help others!" Trusting God is the first three steps, cleaning house involves four through eleven and helping others comes last as **the** result of the first eleven.

Step 1, we touched on earlier but it bears a deeper look. It is said that this is the only step that requires perfection. It is also in two parts. Part one is the admission of powerlessness. Bill Cosby used to do a routine where he was imitating his wife and said something like, "Don't roll your eyes at me, I brought you into this world I can take you out!" It was a hilarious routine and showed the exasperation of a mother dealing with a regular kid and feeling somewhat "powerless." No one wants to admit a loss of control and parents wake up one day to find that they have no power over their offspring anymore; it is an eye opener of epic proportions. All parents experience this and if your kids are "normal" it might not be until your first grandchild is on the way until that powerlessness hits home. For parents of addicts it happens way early in the cycle of life, because addiction really warps that cycle.

Step 2 is the part where we believe in that something unseen, but for some that doesn't work right away. So the power greater than you, for the moment, can be your Alanon group or church group because, just like addicts by this point you may have misplaced your faith in God. So enlist the power in numbers of the others you seek comfort with.

To be restored to sanity implies you ain't all there currently and many of you would not disagree with that statement. The restoration comes from the higher power or better stated, God as you understand Him.

Step 3 brings us to decision making time. Understand, you have not done anything other than confirm you are willing to have God take on all your woes concerning your loved one. You will have the opportunity later to actually turn your will over to God but for now you are just becoming OK with the idea.

This really tests a person's faith. Do we trust God only when we understand what He is up to? I have certainly been guilty of that many times. **Steps 1-3** are designed to bolster that faith, or "Trust God." One should feel better simply by making the necessary opening of their heart and mind to willingness and now it is time to "Clean House."

Now at the **4th Step** it can get hairy and scary. Can you take an **honest inventory of yourself?** Can you look back and take ownership of the things you have done wrong? Can you forgive the wrong that has been done to you? Can you look directly in the eye of your character defects and deal with them? Are you willing to tell your darkest secret to another human being and God? If you answer no to any of the above, go back to steps 1-3 and start over. These are the actions necessary for your addicted loved one to take and so must you.

Having made our list it is time to share it before God with another human being. And so we find ourselves at **Step 5**. A word of caution should be implemented here in this day and age where confidentiality seems to have waivered in many arenas. Please be careful in whom you choose to share your innermost inventory. It is suggested that you find someone who has dealt with their own offspring or loved ones addiction longer than you have, for you will normally find that what seems unforgivable in your mind is really not that shocking at all to the person you are trusting to share your inventory with.

If you can get through **Step 5**, then you are ready to have God remove your character defects. You may say, "Of course I want them removed!" To which I would have to caution you, "not so fast." You see, we have become comfortable in those defects, we've had them all along and now you're being asked to part with them. We like the option to act out on our anger. We like that compromising and rationalizing part of us that can justify things we know are wrong and who doesn't like being victimized once in awhile which justifies a pity party that we can throw for ourselves wallow in it all alone for awhile? I know I do, but **Step 6** is about being "ready" to have God remove these defects. So take a little time and make sure you are ready, before moving to **Step 7** and asking God to remove them.

Once sure you have become ready go directly to Step 7, pass go and jump right in and ask God to take those pesky defects away, then let Him keep them. You will take them back from time to time but eventually you will give them up and not want them back. Now on to **Step 8**.

This is another one of those steps that stalls you long enough to make an assessment. You make a list of all persons you have harmed and trust me, if you are not an addict your list will be shorter than one who has lived a life of addiction. After making the list, you became willing, haven't done it yet nor should you, to make amends to them all.

You have to give this list a whole lot of consideration and remember, you may have harmed someone in a self defense type of situation, like "they said this so I said that." Doesn't matter who started the harming, if you harmed someone, amends is in order and at the very least they should be listed. So once again we are not concerned with what someone did on their side of the street, we are concerned about cleaning up our side. So make the list and take time to reflect.

Step 9, "Made amends to such people wherever possible, except when to do so would injure them or others." A lot said in that sentence. First of all to make amends does not mean you run around telling people you are sorry, not entirely anyway. No, to amend means to change and change means whatever treatment you are responsible for prior to this step to any person, you have changed and were wrong and because you have amended your ways, they should not expect that behavior again.

Secondly, confession is truly good for the soul, but not at someone else's expense. Here is an example of say trying to make amends to your ex-wife that is not acceptable, "Honey please accept my apologies and I have changed and wouldn't do this now, but when we were married I slept with your best friend." You see the problem with that? Whereas you might feel a burden lessened you just laid the burden on two other people. The Big Book of Alcoholics Anonymous and the book The Twelve Steps and Twelve Traditions of AA are both good resources to find instruction on amending your ways.

Step 10 is one of my favorites because it is a step I take every night with God. It is a daily inventory and it keeps those defects on a tight rein and short list if you catch them daily. So when I go to bed I go over my day with God. I look at the things I did well, in my opinion and the things I could have improved. Nothing like having the Ultimate Authority checking these things off with you. Then what happens is you can recognize when you may have harmed or offended some one and quickly correct the mistake and then you are not building another 4th Step. This also ties directly into **Step 11**.

Sought through prayer and meditation to improve our conscious contact with God as we understood Him, praying only for knowledge of His will for us and the power to carry that out. When you can establish that contact with God, your life takes such a powerful and positive turn for the better that words escape me in trying to explain it so just trust me.

Step 12 concerns a spiritual awakening as **"the"** result of these steps. This tells us that this was the goal, to have that spiritual awakening. Now it is time to put these steps and principles in your life and help others coming behind you with the same struggles you had before the steps. This is the step that says basically to get up and do something.

There folks, is a thumbnail explanation of the miraculous 12 Steps. It is for you to study them and apply them to your life in a way that fits you and God. These truly are simple steps, so please don't complicate them. Simple, but difficult to apply, but dear ones, if I can do it, anyone can and I did, with God's help.

Yes My Kid

Chapter 8 Hard Stuff

Now empowered with the 12 Steps and a support group, one can make the difficult decisions about their addicted loved ones without condemning oneself to hell fire and damnation. One has to utilize these tools daily, however; because we have short memories on God trust and like to take our problems back from Him. What hard decisions do I speak of? You're not going to like it but keep reading just the same.

Imagine for a moment you are a bird. Imagine you are a mother bird and while dad is out scouting for worms and bugs and such, you are at home in your comfortable nest with the little baby birds. They are such a joy and you love them dearly even when they seem to only want from you, what you can feed them. You love them because you know, this is the way it is and you have an inborn mother's love. The mother bird embraces every moment for she knows that it won't be long before she has to make the decision.

She looks over at a neighboring nest and sees the mother in solemn tears and she knows the cause of her sorrow. The day before the neighboring mother bird faced the time in every bird's life cycle, the time to push her babies out of the nest that they may learn to fly and become birds on their own. She cries because out of 5 baby birds she pushed out, only four flew back as birds in flight. One, sadly, was unable to take on flight or life. This fact makes the mother bird hesitant to push her own from the nest and yet, she must.

So it is for parents. Like it or not, at some point the umbilical has to be cut and it becomes time for the child to fly or fall, it is no longer in your control. For parents of addicts, this becomes a really tough decision. The hope is that you can hold on to them until they are better, and then let them go. The truth is that by holding on to them, you are not allowing them to get better, you are prolonging their sickness.

Ok parents and loved ones of addicts, here are some truths. Long before you realize what is going on drug-wise with those you love, they have become extremely adept at the art of manipulation. They can play you like a fiddle and you will cry at the melody. Kids will divide their parents and conquer. Addicted spouses will make their partner believe all is their fault. What can I say; addicts should have a category at the Oscars.

Another truth is that you don't want to know the whole truth and nothing but the truth because, believe me, you won't be able to handle what hits you. Know that your loved one has crossed lines you do not want to follow them over and leave it at that. You know enough already to deal with the problem and by dealing with the problem I go back to, at some point, you have to divorce yourself from said problem, which would be your loved ones addiction.

You truly have to be able to allow your loved ones to hate you, if it means that ultimately they will get help. You have to be willing to call the police and allow the consequences to take place. You have to be willing to invest in changing the locks on your doors and securing your house against intrusion. You have to be able to throw these and more road blocks up in the direct path the addict's road to destruction.

You will need God in close conscious contact and human support, as you face down the demons your loved one is in grips of, on a daily basis. None of this is easy and I know you didn't ask for these trials and tribulations but they are in fact Biblically sound:

James 1:2-6
My brethren, count it all joy when you fall into various trials, knowing that the testing of your faith produces patience. But let patience have its perfect work, that you may be perfect and complete, lacking nothing. If

any of you lacks wisdom, let him ask of God, who gives to all liberally and without reproach, and it will be given to him. But let him ask in faith, with no doubting, for he who doubts is like a wave of the sea driven and tossed by the wind.

That is one of my go to chapters in the Bible, for when I have exhausted all my humanly means, I can rest assured that God has it all in His hands.

I could continue to beat you over the head with the hard stuff but all one needs to know is that there is nothing pretty, nothing glamorous, nothing popular about addiction and even less so about you the survivors of those who carry the disease, but it is most assuredly your duty to yourself to take on the problems it causes you, not to fix the problems that inflict them. Keep your eyes, ears, mind and heart vertical and let God handle the horizontal.

Yes My Kid

Chapter 9 Yes My Kid the Program

"Yes My Kid" was one of those plans God had that He felt not compelled to consult me on. Had God asked me, I would have responded, "I am not the right guy!" But He didn't so here am I writing about a program that I would not have started had God not shoved me into action.

It all began with my dad. He had a neighbor who writes Op-Ed for the Columbia Flier, a local weekly newspaper that goes out into Howard County, Maryland. He encouraged me to contact her about my first book, <u>From Junk to Jesus, in the Blink of an Eye</u>. So I did and she was kind enough to write a story. In the story she mentioned my book of course, but also that I attended Grace Community Church. Well a member of Grace, who happened to be a mother and happened to have a son that was struggling with substance abuse, got a copy of my book and read it and then contacted me. So we met and she told me the book had given her a little insight on her son but she desired to know more and what I thought she could do to help him.

From that we started meeting at the church. Before long another mother joined us, then a dad and so on and now in Maryland there are 3 churches to date, that have a "Yes My Kid" program in their ministry arsenals. That is a short summary; it is a bit more complicated in reality.

Churches are made of people, hopefully sharing a love for Christ and following His lead on being open arms to those that hurt. It is a rare occasion when I find a church where that is not the message coming from the pulpit, but there are times when the translation from the pulpit to the people get skewed. We, and when I say we I mean me too, go to church and it can be a euphoric experience. Everyone smiles, hugs and gives authentic praises and my how the churches can look so downright pristine it is difficult not to feel good. Throw in a good coffee bar and Starbuck's has trouble competing on Sunday mornings. We just feel great and woe be to anyone who would rain on this gala Sunday parade by mentioning a troubled loved one. Yet on any given Sunday, every other family, at least, in the pews or folding chairs or plush theater seating, has someone close to them struggling with addiction, even some of the pastors, elders and deans.

So why is it that we have so much trouble addressing the demons of addiction in church? We certainly take no issue when we learn about the Aids Epidemic in Africa, or we take up prayer for those lost in terrible natural disasters and we will bang the gong loudly to come up with support for cancer and all are righteous and just causes, but I submit that so is addiction and if we consider Jesus the Physician are we right to sweep substance abuse under the plush carpeted foyer of our church? I think not. Sadly, we do.

This leaves it to us to take up the cross and carry it to the church. By this I mean I have yet to run into a church that would not support a ministry once the need is pointed out and once enough people express that need. In defense of the churches powers that be, they get bombarded with great ideas from well intended parishioners daily and for them to give credence to them all is not possible. That is why; if one feels the need for a support group for parents in any given church it is up to them to make it so.

We at IBE Ministries, Inc. formed "Yes My Kid." We implemented it at Grace Community Church until a leader rose up from within the support group and then IBE backed away and the church took up the ministry and made it their own. This happen in two other churches by word of mouth, the first spin-off, if you will, was Friendship Baptist Church in Sykesville, MD, followed not long after by Cedar Ridge Community Church in Burtonsville, MD.

As with any ministry, there have been great stories of recovery and hope and others not so much of the same. All one needs to get this going is the belief that there is a need, a Bible and a space. IBE Ministries will implement the program and get it up and running as we have done in the past and then gladly turn over the reins to the church at a suitable time as to be determined by the members of the support group and of course a time when God blesses it so.

The "Yes My Kid" program and IBE Ministries, involvement comes at no cost. It might be necessary for the church to pay for startup materials and other such minor expenses and IBE is always open to donations as we are a charitable organization, but the costs are minimum if existent at all. This book has not been written as an attempt to profit off something we have given our best effort for the greater good, but merely to make available a valuable support tool for victims that addicts, like me, leave in their wake.

Yes My Kid

In Closing

Dear ones, I hope that from these pages you can draw some useful information to navigate the extremely rocky roads addictions will take you on. I envy you not. Yours is the toughest of trials but there is hope. I want to reassure you that whomever you love that is now addicted, **it is not your fault**. Scientifically it can be said and has been said that this disease would have been set in motion by the first drink or drug, no matter what the upbringing of the child entailed, not matter what abuse the child may have experienced and no matter how much you hugged and loved them. It is what it is, a powerful and all encompassing disease of the brain.

So beat yourselves up no more. Take action to increase your spiritual fitness, you are going to need all the help you and God can put together. Turn your loved one over to the care of God and rest assured He knows what He is doing and trust me, when it comes to addiction, you don't know what you are doing. Draw on the experiences of others, who trudged the rocky road before you, they can help you avoid the deep ruts and chasms.

Remember, the father of the prodigal son did not go chasing after him, but he welcomed him home with great fanfare. So must you wait, not chase, so must you shove your little bird out of the nest and pray God give them the wings to fly, so must you be fervent in prayer and meditation for your own peace. Barring these things and not taking these steps you are committed to living in misery. If you want something different, you must be willing to do something different. I will leave you with one final prayer that in AA is called the 11th Step Prayer:

"Lord make me a channel of thy peace -- that where there is hatred, I may bring love -- that where there is wrong, I may bring the spirit of forgiveness -- that where there is discord, I may bring harmony -- that where there is error, I may bring truth -- that where there is doubt, I may bring faith -- that where there is despair, I may bring hope -- that where there are shadows, I may bring light -- that where there is sadness, I may bring joy.

Lord, grant that I may seek rather to comfort than to be comforted -- to understand, than to be understood -- to love, than to be loved.

For it is by self-forgetting that one finds. It is by forgiving that one is forgiven. It is by dying that one awakens to Eternal Life... *Saint Francis*

Program Instructions

The following is an outline on how you can proceed if you feel your church, group or even place of business or school would benefit from the Yes My Kid Program.

- Establish the need for YMK. If you can find one other person who shares your concern and confusion of what to do about a loved one on the path of drug destruction, then you have your need. The two of you get together and share who else you might think benefit.

- Contact me, John Michael Weber at jmichael@intheblinkofaneyeministries.com and express your desire to start a group. I will get contact info for your church and send you start up materials including a DVD that introduces non-addicts to addiction. We can then discuss how IBE can help you implement and facilitate this program in your venue.

- Ask your church for a room you can meet in for an hour and a half in the evening or on weekends. You will need access to chairs and a TV with a DVD player.

- Have a couple of meetings by word of mouth before you ask the church to publish the meeting in your bulletin. It is very important that once you begin, you do not stop. AA never cancels a meeting unless the place is unreachable due to natural disasters and you need to be driven by the same commitment. You don't want to advertise this and then not show up the one week a desperate parent decides to give it a shot.

- Make sure that you have a Bible, a Big Book of Alcoholics Anonymous and perhaps current events involving substance abuse locally and nationally, they make for good discussions.

- When it becomes clear that the group is the real deal, then you approach the church or board of education or whoever makes the thumbs up or down decisions and ask that YMK become part of the church, school or company.

- When dealing with a church it will be important you approach the right person and have your ducks in a row before you go in to present the idea. Most churches will want an elder or pastor to sit in a group or two to make sure you are not in violation of the church doctrine, this is fine, welcome them.

- When you get an ok, then IBE bows out gracefully and YMK becomes your churches ministry. We will always be available for consult, but this allows you to make the program fit the specific needs of your venue.

- As far as schools and businesses, good luck. We are a faith based charitable non-profit and consider the Bible the main source of your restoration and that does not bode well in secular settings. That being said, try it anyway.

Well there you have it folks. I always struggle writing books. Did I make it too long, too short, leave something out, mention something twice, things of that nature drive me crazy. I am still stopping right here for I think at the very least I am leaving you with something to mull over.

Nothing about drug addiction is easy, nothing. It is a life of seemingly hopeless misery for the addict and seemingly hopeless fear for those who love them. Getting help can be expensive and in the case of adolescents getting help at all is troublesome and I am being nice. Look for another book sometime in the future about the frustrations counselors face trying to help addicts, it is grotesquely riddled with the most ludicrous rules, regulations and barriers of futility that are unimaginable and truthfully it revolves around money. Doesn't everything?

You, dear ones, like my daughters and parents and anyone I knew, are my heroes for praying for people like me. You are my heroes for living daily lives as they come at you and being responsible even while fearing the outcome of your loved ones. We get rewarded in AA for periods of sobriety. We get applause for paying our electric bills on time. We celebrate, just to clarify, so that someone new coming in can see that there is hope for a better life. So it seems somewhat unfair to me, that you people rarely get applause for just living life on life's terms. It reminds me of what my principal in eighth grade once said over the loud speakers one fine day, "Do not expect to get rewarded for something you should be doing anyway." I can't tell you much about my junior high years but that one little piece of profound proverbial prose stuck with me all these years.

There is hope for all as long as they are breathing. If I can change, anyone can change and ask anyone, I changed.

"I can do all things through Christ who strengthens me."
Philippians 4:13 Amen!

The End

About the Author

John Michael Weber was born on May 14, 1958 in Texas City, Texas. By 12 years old he was on a journey to addiction that would leave damage in his wake for anyone close to him and some that weren't.

Today with over ten years clean and sober, to date, Mr. Weber is a Chaplain, published author of four previous books and an addictions counselor in the same area of Texas where he began his addiction, Mr. Weber sees everyday in other parents, the pain he caused to his own for some thirty plus years.

John Michael Weber now resides in Seabrook, Texas he has two daughters Lindsey Nicole and Lauren Elizabeth Weber, with whom he is blessed with a great relationship and a granddaughter, Elizabeth Renee Witherspoon and a grandson on the way to boot.

He is president and founder of IBE Ministries, Inc., a 501c3 charitable nonprofit dedicated to providing solutions, care and hope to families that struggle with substance abuse and addiction. IBE Ministries, Inc is vessel that carried "Yes My Kid" into churches.

IBE Center
for
Solutions, Care & Hope
1001 West H Street, Suite B
La Porte, TX 77571
www.intheblinkofaneyeministries.com
281-515-6673

Other Books by John Michael Weber

From Junk to Jesus, In the Blink of an Eye

From Junk to Jesus, Ponders, Passions & Poems

The UnHoly Trinity, Me, Myself, & I

Preacher (Fiction)

For the Online Store:
http://www.lulu.com/spotlight/weberdfcatyahoodotcom